SO-EIF-061

CASH FOR COLLEGE

How To Send Your Kids
To The College
Of Their Dreams
And Not Go Broke

by Daniel J. Wansten, M.Ed., MBA

Copyright Notice

©   2001   Professional Education Services
      2004   2nd Printing Dickinson Press
ISBN 0-9758770-0-3

All rights reserved.

Any unauthorized transfer of license, use, sharing, reproduction, or
distribution of these materials by any means, electronic, mechanical, or
otherwise is strictly prohibited. No portion of these materials may be
reproduced in any manner whatsoever, without the express written
consent of the publishers.

Published under the Copyright Laws of the Library of Congress of
the United States of America, by
Professional Education Services
2828 Kraft Avenue SE, Suite 202
Grand Rapids, MI   49512
(616) 949-7935
collegefunding49546@yahoo.com

Legal Notices
While all attempts have been made to verify information provided in this
publication, neither the Author nor the Publisher assumes any
responsibility for errors, omissions, or contradictory interpretation of the
subject matter herein.

The publication is not intended for use as a source of legal or accounting
advice. The publishers want to stress that the information contained
herein may be subject to varying state and/or local laws or regulations.
All users are advised to retain competent counsel to determine what state
and/or local laws or regulations may apply to the user's particular
situation.

---

*The purchaser or reader of this publication assumes responsibility for the
use of these materials and information. Adherence to all applicable laws
and regulations, both federal and state, and local, governing professional
licensing, business practices, advertising and all other aspects of doing
business in the United States or any other jurisdiction is the sole
responsibility of the purchaser or reader. Daniel Wansten and Professional
Education Services assumes no responsibility or liability whatsoever on
the behalf of any purchaser or reader of these materials.*

IMPORTANT!
READ THIS FIRST!

Dear Parent,

Your decision to get this book is probably going to turn out to be the smartest financial move you've ever made!

As you're about to discover, this book totally delivers on every single promise I've made in my advertising. Not only that, every money-saving idea and strategy you are about to read has already been tested and proven to work. These ideas have already saved parents just like you, $1,000's, and in some cases, $10,000's of dollars on their children's college educations.

Consider This: The secrets revealed in Chapter #1 will show you how to avoid making the 10 deadliest mistakes most parents make when applying for college funding.

And This: The secret in Chapter #6 will reveal the 8 vital questions you must ask colleges before applying for financial aid. (Failure to ask any one of these questions could cost you a fortune!)

And This: The secret revealed in Chapter #9 that will show you how to negotiate the best possible financial aid package for your child. (Yes, you really can negotiate with colleges and get $2,000 - $5,000 **more per year** just by knowing how to do this!)

And This: The secrets in the other 11 chapters should remove almost every other mental or financial roadblock that has prevented you from thinking you can afford to send your child to the college of their choice.

Now Listen: Somewhere along the line, you're going to realize the information in this book is literally worth thousands of dollars, and you're going to wonder why I'm revealing all of these inside secrets for FREE.

The reason is rather interesting. You see, I offer a fee-based college financial aid planning service that helps parents send their child to the college of their choice without spending their life's savings.

And guess what? In spite of my fee, almost every parent who becomes a client of mine decides to have me help them for all 4 years their child is in college, and many of them end up using my services for all of their children, and referring me to all of their friends and relatives.

Why, you ask? Simply because my college funding service saves parents anywhere from $6,000 - $60,000 per child on their family college costs!

However, sometimes a parent has to "sample the merchandise" before they can tell how valuable my services are, and not everyone is willing to use my service unless they have already seen some of my information. Therefore, I've decided to include some of my best college funding ideas and strategies in this book so you can discover for yourself just how valuable my information really is. And then, after you've read the rest of this book, you'll discover in Chapter #15, how you can become a client of mine and also...

How To Send Your Child To The College Of Their Choice Without Spending Your Life's Savings...<u>GUARANTEED</u>!

Anyway, it's up to you. Even if you decide <u>not</u> to use my college funding service, you will still have received the bargain of a lifetime getting this book for only $29.95. And, on the other hand, if you're truly serious about sending your child to the college of their choice <u>without</u> spending your life's savings, you may very well decide to use my college funding service so you can also save $1,000's of dollars <u>per year</u> on your child's college education — <u>GUARANTEED</u>!

Yours In College Funding Success,
Daniel Wansten

P.S.   You'll benefit more if you read this book straight through from beginning to end instead of "hopping around" from one section to another.

Enjoy!

ABOUT THE AUTHOR

Daniel Wansten is one of the nation's leading authorities for college funding solutions.

Daniel founded Professional Education Services in 1999 with his wife Rebecca. Daniel educates people through community sponsored workshops and individual meetings. He has helped thousands of parents send their children to college without spending their life's savings or mortgaging their house to the hilt! Daniel is an ordained minister who is committed to the highest ethical standards of business and community service. He has been helping to solve family financial issues for over 20 years.

Daniel Wansten is a highly sought after speaker and media favorite with his insider's secrets on how to legally beat the high cost of college.

Daniel Wansten knows the college funding challenge. In fact He himself has over 14 years of college and graduate school. Daniel holds a Bachelors degree from North Central University, a Masters Degree in Education from Cornerstone University and in addition he holds a MBA and PhD in Finance from Columbus University. He is the former President of North American Financial Corporation. Daniel is a full member of the "Who's Who" Historical Society of International Professionals.

Daniel Wansten makes his home in Cascade, MI. with his spouse, Rebecca, and four children, two of whom are in college. He is a firm believer that any parent, regardless of their background or financial circumstances, can send their child to college if they know how to play the financial aid game properly. Daniel Wansten is a member of the National Association of College Funding Advisors.

For more information concerning upcoming college funding workshops, or to schedule an appointment for a FREE financial aid consultation,...simply call for more information at (616) 949-7935.

If you would like to have Daniel speak to your High School, or at your Public Library, or Community Group call (616) 949-7935. Be sure to mention that you got this number from Daniel's book.

Table of Contents

Chapter 1   10 Deadliest Mistakes 1

Chapter 2   4 Little-Known Reasons 9

Chapter 3   A Checklist 15

Chapter 4   7 Things To Do Right Now 21

Chapter 5   How To Pick A College 27

Chapter 6   8 Vital Questions 35

Chapter 7   What You Must Do 41

Chapter 8   How To Take Control 47

Chapter 9   How To Negotiate 55

Chapter 10   Warning!!! 61

Chapter 11   How To Get Maximum Money 67

Chapter 12   5 Little-Known Secrets 73

Chapter 13   A Treasure Chest 79

Chapter 14   9 New Secrets 85

Chapter #1

"The 10 Deadliest Mistakes Most Parents Make When Applying For College Funding-- And How To Avoid Them..."

We're going to start by talking about the 10 deadliest mistakes almost every parent makes when trying to get money for their child's college education.

If you make any one of these mistakes, it could end up costing you thousands or even tens of thousands of dollars in lost funding that you might have been eligible for.

I don't want to see you making these mistakes if you don't have to. That's why I've decided to devote this chapter to teaching you how to avoid these common mistakes and make sure you get the maximum amount of money from every school your child applies to.

So, without further ado, let's discuss...

**"The 10 Deadliest Mistakes Most Parents Make
When Applying For College Funding..."**

Here they are:

Mistake #1: **Most middle and upper-middle
class parents assume they won't be eligible for
financial aid because they own a home and make
over $50,000 per year.**

Reality: Most families with incomes ranging from
$50,000 - $150,000 per year who own homes are
eligible for some form of financial aid. There is
over 30 billion dollars available each year from the
Federal Government, the states, colleges and
universities, and private foundations and
organizations. You just have to know how to get
your "fair share". Unfortunately, most parents give
up before they even start and assume they won't be
eligible. This is exactly what the government hopes
you will do so they can keep more of these funds.
Don't make this mistake! If you fall into this
category, make sure you apply; you'll probably be
eligible for SOME money.

Mistake #2: **Focusing your time and energy on
a private scholarship search instead of spending
your time trying to qualify for "need-based"
financial aid.**

Reality: Private scholarships make up only 3% of the money available to you to help pay for your child's college education. The other 97% comes from the Federal Government, the state you live in, and the colleges and universities your child is applying to. Therefore, you are much better off spending your time and energy going after the 97%, rather than spending your time on the 3%.

Mistake #3:   Assuming only minority students, athletes, and academically gifted students get financial aid.

Reality: Nothing could be further from the truth! "Need-based" financial aid is solely awarded based on "financial need" which is calculated by taking the cost of attendance at a school and subtracting the family contribution (which is the minimum amount the government feels you can afford to pay based on your income and assets and your child's income and assets). Whatever is left over after you subtract these two numbers is your "financial need" or eligibility for financial aid at a particular school. If you haven't noticed, this has nothing to do with a student's ethnic background, athletic ability, or grades. It's purely based on this simple formula:

COA (Cost Of Attendance)
- FC (Family Contribution)
= FN (Financial Need)

Mistake #4: **Picking colleges and universities without paying attention to where your student lies in comparison to the rest of the student body.**

<u>Reality</u>: To increase your chances of getting the best possible financial aid packages, it is imperative that you pick schools where your child lies in the top 10% of the incoming freshman class with respect to their GPA and SAT/ACT scores. Although schools give financial aid based on your calculation of "need" at their school, they will definitely give preferential packaging (i.e., more FREE money, less loans) to students who lie in the top 10% of the incoming class. The reason they do this is to attract the better students to their school. Use this to your advantage and apply <u>only</u> to those schools where your child would fit into the top 10% category.

Mistake #5: **Assuming all schools are created equal and will be able to give you the same amounts of money.**

<u>Reality</u>: All schools are <u>not</u> created equal and will <u>not</u> be able to give you the same financial aid packages. Some schools are well endowed and get a lot of money from alumni and corporations. These schools have more money to give out and are generally able to meet most or all of a student's financial need at their school. Other schools, like state universities, get no private funds and rely solely on state and Federal funds to help fill a

student's need at their school. In many cases, these schools leave students short and give them less money than they are eligible to receive. It can actually end up costing you more to send your child to a "cheaper" school if they don't have the money to meet your need. It is very important that you know each school's history of giving money before you ever apply, so you're not blown away when you get a bad financial aid package from your child's top school choice.

Mistake #6:   Not understanding the difference between "included assets" and "un-included assets" for purposes of filling out financial aid forms.

Reality: Certain assets are counted much more heavily in the financial aid formulas than others. For example, savings accounts, CD's, stocks and bonds are <u>all</u> included and asked about on the Federal Financial Aid form. However, it <u>does</u> <u>not</u> ask about the value of annuities or cash-value life insurance anywhere on that same form.

Mistake #7:   It doesn't matter where I keep my money; it's all counted in the same way.

Reality: Nothing could be further from the truth. Where you keep your money could mean the difference between you getting $10,000 in financial aid or getting nothing! For example, money in the child's name is weighted much more heavily than money in the parent's name. If you don't know how to legally and ethically position your money properly for purposes of financial aid, you could end up losing thousands in financial aid!

Mistake #8: **"My CPA or tax preparer is qualified to fill out my financial aid forms - I'll let him/her do it."**

Reality: Unfortunately, CPA's and tax preparers are experts at tax planning and preparation - not financial aid planning. For example, a CPA or tax preparer might suggest that you put some or all of your assets in your child's name to save money on taxes. While this advice is well meaning, it will usually kill most or all of your chances of getting financial aid. Also, CPA's and tax preparers are not trained in filling out financial aid forms. In many cases, they will unknowingly fill out these forms improperly (i.e., using pen instead of pencil, using white-out to cover mistakes, omitting social security numbers, etc.), and these "minor" mistakes will bump your financial aid forms. If this happens, you will have to re-submit these forms all over again, and you will probably end up losing thousands in financial aid since it is awarded on a first come, first served basis.

Mistake #9: **Waiting until January or even worse after January of your child's senior year of high school to start working on your college financial aid planning.**

Reality: Since financial aid is based on your previous year's income and assets, it is imperative to start your planning as soon as possible before January of your child's senior year. If you want to legally set up your income and assets so you can maximize your eligibility for financial aid, you must start working on this, at least, one year in advance - preferably in the beginning of your child's JUNIOR year of high school. The longer you wait and the closer it gets to your child's senior year, the tougher it gets to set up your financial picture without creating a "red flag" for the colleges and universities. It is also important for you to know what your **"Expected Family Contribution"** is so you can start saving for it. And, you should also know which schools can give you the best packages before you start visiting and applying to them. My advice is if you haven't started planning, DO IT NOW!

Mistake #10: Going Through The Financial Aid Process By Yourself Because It's "Cheaper".

Reality: If this describes you, the colleges and Federal Government are going to love you! This allows them to keep control over the process instead of you, the parent, understanding how the process works and taking back control from them.

7

It always amazes me that people will readily use a doctor when they get sick, a lawyer when they get sued, but suddenly when they are going to send their child to college and spend between $14,000 - $35,000 <u>per</u> <u>year</u>, parents want to save themselves a couple of dollars and do it themselves.

Unless you spent the last 5 - 10 years of your life studying and understanding the financial aid process, there is no way you are going to know how to get the maximum amount of money from each school. And, if you do try it yourself, you'll probably spend countless hours trying to figure it out.

The moral to this story is:

"Don't Be Penny Wise And Dollar Foolish!"

Use an expert who can help you through this process and make sure you get everything you're entitled to.

Chapter #2

"4 Little-Known Reasons Why You Should Start Planning For Your Child's College Education NOW - Even If You Have No Idea What Schools They Want To Apply To..."

Most families (and people in general) wait until the absolute last minute to do everything.

That's why very few people end up financially prepared to pay for weddings, homes, retirement, and college educations for their children.

Well, since we only have a limited amount of space and considering the focus of this book is college funding - we're going to discuss 4 little-known reasons why you should start planning for your child's college education in their JUNIOR year of high school (if not earlier).

Reason #1:   Money Saved In The Wrong Places Could Cost You A Fortune In Lost Financial Aid.

Did you know that money saved in the wrong places could count as much as 7 times more heavily than money saved in the right places?

It is important that you determine which assets you have accumulated in the "wrong" places so you can either gift, transfer or reposition them <u>before</u> you have to apply for financial aid.

If you wait until the last minute to do this (your child's senior year), it will be too late to change your financial picture, and you will end up losing thousands of dollars in financial aid that you would have been eligible for.

Reason #2:   You Must Know How Much Your Family Will Be Expected To Contribute Towards College Costs.

No matter which schools your child ends up applying to, the government will expect you to pay your fair share towards the cost of college. They call this your **"Expected Family Contribution"** and this is the minimum amount of money <u>any</u> school will expect you to pay towards your child's education.

The sooner you know what this number is, the sooner you can start saving to accumulate at least enough to cover this minimum amount.

If you wait until your child's senior year of high school to find out what your family contribution is, you will have no time to do any saving - and this means borrowing more money to cover the costs of your child's college education!

Reason #3: You Want Your Child To Pick Schools Based On The Schools Ability To Give You Money.

Most students and parents pick schools whimsically without giving any consideration to which schools have the best ability to meet their financial needs.

What happens is that most students start picking schools towards the end of their junior year, visit them during the summer, and then start applying to them in their senior year of high school.

The entire process is very costly between travel and application expenses, and most students and parents are stunned at the end of their senior year when they find out there is no way they can afford most of the schools they applied to!

This scenario can easily be avoided by finding out which schools have the best histories of giving good financial aid packages - more FREE money, less loans!

By finding out this information in your child's JUNIOR year of high school, you can avoid spending time and money traveling and applying to schools that will <u>never</u> be able to give you the money you need.

<u>Reason #4</u>: You Must Start, At Least, One Year In Advance If You Want To Apply For Private Scholarships.

Although private scholarships only make up 1% of all the money that exists for college funding, it still can be worth looking for some of these funding sources.

Private Scholarships are sources of FREE money that never have to be re-paid.

Private foundations and organizations offer them to students based on their ethnic background, religious affiliation, talents, hobbies, skills, interests, athletic abilities, etc.

You can only get these sources of funding if you apply for them, and you can only locate and apply for them if you start looking in your child's JUNIOR year of high school.

* * *

These 4 little-known reasons could mean the difference between you getting thousands of dollars in college funding or not being able to afford to send your child to the college or university of his/ her choice.

Chapter #3

"A Checklist Of Things You Should Be Doing <u>Right</u> <u>Now</u> If You're The Parent Of A College-Bound High School Junior..."

In this chapter, we're going to discuss things you should be doing <u>right</u> <u>now</u> if your child is nearing the end of his or her junior year of high school.

But, before I tell you what you should do, I'd like to tell you what you <u>shouldn't</u> <u>do</u>...

Don't Get Lulled Into A False Sense Of Security!

Most parents (and people) get a strange disease called "summer fever" right around when the weather starts getting nice again.

Symptoms include leaving work early, taking half-day Fridays, playing golf and tennis, being more active than usual, and...

Blowing Off Every Important Financial Decision Until <u>After</u> The Summer's Over!

This is usually a big mistake. Panic attacks and nervous episodes start occurring sometime in August as a result of this.

Don't Let This Happen To You!

Don't misunderstand me. Go out and enjoy your summer. Live life to the fullest. Take long weekends and vacations.

But, don't forget to start planning for your child's college education!

<u>Here's a checklist of things you should be doing right now if you're the parent of a college-bound high-school junior</u>:

1. **<u>Start Visiting Colleges And Universities That Your Child Is Interested In Applying To</u>.**

Most high school students base their decisions on where they want to go to college on "word of mouth". They listen to what their friends say is a good school, or they consult college guides, magazines, and guidance counselors.

Whichever way they decide on their college choices, they must visit the campuses of these schools first to get a good feeling for what each school is like.

Do they want a small town or big city environment? Big or small class sizes? Fraternities or sororities? Good weather or bad weather? What are the people on campus like - cool, nerdy, whatever?

These questions can only be answered by visiting the schools, and now is the time to do it before they apply.

2.   <u>Have Your Child Take A Good Test Preparation Course To Get A Better SAT Score.</u>

The good colleges are getting more and more competitive. If they receive applications from two students with the exact same grades and similar extra-curricular activities...

Guess Who They're Gonna Pick?

If you guessed the student with the higher SAT scores, you were right.

Sometimes a higher SAT score can make <u>all</u> the difference between getting into an "O.K." school and a prestigious university.

The small investment you make in a good test preparation service will pay off in high returns for your child.

3. <u>Start Looking For Private Scholarships</u>.

I'm not a big believer in wasting a whole lot of time searching for private scholarships since they only make up about 3% of all the funds available for a college education.

But, just like the lottery - "you gotta get in it to win it!"

Have your child ask their high school guidance counselor what local scholarships are available, and have him/her get applications for all the programs that they think they have a shot at.

4. <u>Start Setting Up Your Income, Assets & Personal Finances To Get The Maximum Amount Of Money From Each School</u>.

Do you have money saved in your child's name? Are you planning on putting money into your retirement plan this year? Do you know how much your home is <u>really</u> worth according to the financial aid formulas?

If you're not sure what the answer <u>should</u> <u>be</u> to the above listed questions, you've got to find out!

A simple mistake in how you handle any of the above situations could easily cost you thousands, if not tens of thousands in lost financial aid.

You <u>must</u> take control of the process, and understand how the formula works.

Then, and only then, can you use legal and ethical strategies to reduce the amount of money the schools will expect you to pay.

5. <u>Don't Procrastinate.</u>

This is the <u>most</u> important point on the entire checklist.

If you let "summer fever" take over, and decide to put off doing anything until "after the summer's over"...

You're Gonna Lose A Lot Of Money!

Since the financial aid your child will be awarded is based on the current tax year, it is imperative that you start your planning <u>NOW</u>!

Failure to do so <u>WILL</u> cost you a lot of money and lost opportunities to your child.

Don't make the same mistake that most parents make, and put this planning off until another time.

The Time To Do Something Is Right Now!

Chapter #4

"7 Things You Should Be Doing <u>RIGHT NOW</u> To Get The Maximum Amount Of Money For Your Child's College Education..."

1. <u>Have Your Child Apply To At Least 6 - 8 Colleges And Universities</u>.

Pick an assortment of "safety schools", "competitive schools", and "reach schools".

Try to pick, at least, several schools where your child lies in the top 25% of the incoming freshman class.

Otherwise, there is a good likelihood that the schools won't give you a good financial aid package since your child won't be a desirable candidate.

Also, make sure they apply to more than just 1 or 2 schools even if they're dead set on going to a particular school.

By applying to about 6 - 8 schools, you will greatly increase your ability to negotiate financial aid packages at the end of the year by pitting one school against the other.

2. <u>Figure Out How To Value Your Home Properly</u>.

Most families end up over-valuing their homes for purposes of financial aid. Don't make this mistake - it could cost you thousands of dollars in lost college funding.

Instead, the schools use a special formula called "The Housing Index Multiplier" which is based on your home's original purchase price and the year you purchased it.

Find out what your "multiplier" is and use this value for your home.

3. <u>Do Last Minute Income And Asset Planning To Lower Your Out-Of-Pocket Costs</u>.

You <u>MUST</u> set up your finances in a way that will maximize your eligibility for college financial aid.

Assets held in the wrong place will kill your chances of getting money.

Should a parent or sibling attend college part-time to increase your eligibility?

Are you properly valuing your real estate?

If you're not sure, you'd better find out the answers to these questions quickly before it's too late!

4. <u>Don't Apply For Early Decision If You Want To Get The Maximum Amount Of Money From Each School</u>.

If your child applies for early decision, they are locked into going to that school.

This is a huge mistake if you're trying to get the maximum amount of money for college.

The reality is that if a school knows you <u>have to</u> go to their school if they accept you, they have no competition and can offer you whatever they want.

Therefore, it's a very <u>bad idea</u> to apply for early decision since you have no leverage to negotiate for a better financial aid package.

5. **Find Out Each School's Deadline For The Financial Aid Applications - And Don't Miss A Deadline!**

The earliest date you can file the Federal financial aid application (which is called the FAFSA) is January 1.

However, many private colleges and universities will also ask you to fill out the Financial Aid Profile (FAP). Different schools have different deadlines for this form.

Don't miss a deadline - it will cost you a lot of money in lost financial aid!

6. **Look For Private Sources Of College Funding.**

Don't waste too much time looking for private scholarships since they only make up 3% of all the aid out there, but it's worth spending a little time looking for these sources.

Focus on local awards from foundations, organizations, and corporations. You can usually get more information on these awards from your child's high school guidance counselor.

7. Don't Let a Well Meaning High School Guidance Counselor Or College Financial Aid Officer Give You A False Sense Of Security.

Some high school guidance counselors tell parents, "Don't worry about it - it's an easy process, just fill out the forms and sit back and wait for your award letter."

Unfortunately, it's not that simple!

If you want to get the maximum amount of money from each school, you've got to set up your finances properly, fill out the forms accurately and on-time, and negotiate with colleges and universities to get the best possible financial aid package.

Unfortunately, guidance counselors don't have the time or the training to do these things - so you can't rely on them to help you maximize your eligibility for college funding. That is not their job.

College aid officers may offer to help you apply for financial aid.

But going to a financial aid officer and asking them to help you get more money from their school is like going to the IRS and asking them to help you save money on your taxes!

It's not in a school's best interest to teach you how to get more money from their school. They have a limited number of funds to give out to a large number of people.

Think twice before you let a guidance counselor or college aid officer "help" you apply for college funding - it may turn out to be **<u>a very expensive mistake</u>**!

Chapter #5

"How To Pick A College Or University That Will Give You The Best Financial Aid Package— More FREE Money, Less Loans!"

In this chapter, I'm going to tell you about something that may save you thousands or even tens of thousands of dollars on your child's college education.

Most families take a completely "backwards" approach when searching for money for college.

Normally, the process goes something like this....

In the child's junior (or even worse), senior year of high school, they start picking schools they may be interested in going to, and that they believe they can get into based on their grades, SAT scores, extracurricular activities, etc.

Many students pick a grouping of "safety" schools which they know they can get into, "middle of the range" schools which they have a good shot of getting into, and "reach" schools which they would love to attend, but have a slim chance of getting into.

The next step in the process is that the student starts requesting literature from all of these schools (usually towards the end of their junior year of high school or in the summer preceding their senior year).

Once they receive the literature, most families start planning weekend trips to visit one or more of the schools the student is interested in applying to.

This is how most students and families get a "feel" for each college campus, and determine if they would feel comfortable being a student there.

Just in case you haven't noticed...

All Of This Traveling From Campus To Campus Costs You A Lot Of Time And Money.

It also happens to be the "wrong" way to do things if you want to be in control of the college selection process and get the maximum amount of financial aid from each school.

What most parents and students don't understand is that...

Your Child Will Probably Be Accepted To Approximately 70% Of The Schools They Apply To!

Unless, of course, if your child is a borderline student, and they're applying to the Ivy League or the most competitive schools.

If your child is <u>not</u> applying <u>only</u> to reach schools or the Ivy League...

They Have A Good Shot At Getting Into Most Of The Schools They're Applying To!

You see, it's not like 10 or 20 years ago, when there were more students applying to college than there were available seats.

Today, most colleges are struggling to keep their doors open, and they need students (like your child) to help pay their bills.

It's the old law of supply and demand, and today, the supply of available seats at colleges and universities is greater than the demand to get into these schools.

This is great news for parents. This puts you in the driver's seat if, and only if, you know how to take advantage of this trend.

Do you want to know the "right" way to look for colleges and universities for your child?

You do? Good, then let's continue on.

Instead of blindly picking schools purely based on academic criteria, or sports criteria, or because your friend or relative's son loves a particular college, you must look at one other very important criteria...

Can This School Meet My Family's Financial Need And Give Us More FREE Money And Fewer Loans?

Remember, your child will get into most of the schools he/she is applying to (unless they are reaching for the Ivy's or the most competitive schools).

So the question is <u>not</u>, "Will my child get into this school?" Instead, the right question to ask is, "Will this school be able to give me the money I will need to send my child there for the next 4 years?"

If you haven't realized it yet - college is very expensive these days!

Even a state school can cost you $14,000 or more per year when you include tuition, fees, books, room and board, living expenses, etc.

A private university can easily run you $35,000 per year and more!

And that's just 1 year! Remember, you have 3 more years to go after that. And what about if your child wants to go to graduate school?

It's definitely expensive no matter which way you slice it, but there are ways to minimize these costs.   One of the best ways to do this is by picking schools that historically have the best policies of giving financial aid.

A brief explanation of the financial aid process is necessary for me to explain this to you.

So, here we go.

Financial aid is awarded at each school based on a calculation of a family's "financial need".

Financial need is calculated by subtracting the Family Contribution (this is the minimum amount you will be expected to pay at <u>ANY</u> school) from the "Cost of Attendance" which includes tuition, fees, books, room and board, etc.

So, if a school costs $20,000 and the <u>FEDERAL GOVERNMENT</u> calculates your family contribution to be $10,000, your "need" at that school is $10,000.
It works like this:

$20,000 (Cost of Attendance)
- $10,000 (Family Contribution)
=$10,000 (Financial Need)

Financial need determines how much financial aid your family is eligible to receive. However, just because your need is $10,000, does not mean you will be offered $10,000 at that school.

This is where picking schools that historically give the best financial aid packages come in.

You see some schools can meet 100% of your family's financial need while others will only meet 20% or 30%.

The other thing you must know when picking schools is how much of the "need" they meet in "FREE" money, which you never have to pay back, and how much need they meet in "Self-Help" money, which includes loans that you <u>do</u> have to pay back.

By knowing each school's ability to give financial aid, in advance, you can pick schools that you have the best chance of getting money from.

This puts you, instead of the schools, in control of the process.

By knowing, in advance, which of the schools can meet most of your need, and give you more FREE money and less loans, you will also save yourself the time, energy, and hassle of applying to schools that will <u>never</u> be able to give you the money you need to send your child there.

This type of planning should be done as soon as possible **before your child's senior year** of high school, so you don't end up visiting and applying to colleges you will never be able to afford.

If you're wondering how you can find out about this type of information, you can start by asking the financial aid officer at each school. Some of them will be completely honest about their ability to give money, and others will keep very silent about these numbers.

The other option is to use the services of a college-funding consultant who maintains an updated version of these statistics on a computer database.

Whichever way you decide to do it, make sure you know each college's statistics on meeting your financial need, and typically how much they give in FREE money versus Self-Help (i.e., loans and work study) <u>before</u> applying to them.

Once you know these numbers, you are in the driver's seat, not the schools.

You can also save yourself a lot of time, energy, and money by not applying to or visiting schools that will never give you the money you need to send your child to their institution.

Chapter #6

"8 Vital Questions Every Parent Must Ask Colleges Before Applying For Financial Aid..."

If your child is in his/her senior year of high school and hasn't started filling out their college applications -

Make Sure They Do It Right Now!

You Must Find Out The Financial Aid Deadlines At Each College And Make Sure You Get The Financial Aid Forms In Before The Earliest Deadline!

In addition to getting all your applications in accurately and on-time, you also want to stack the cards in your favor by asking these 8 Vital Questions to the financial aid officer at each school:

Question #1 - **Does your school guarantee to meet 100% of my child's financial need at your school, and if not, what percentage of need does your school meet for the average student?**

Most schools do <u>not</u> meet 100% of a student's financial need. It is important for you to know this information, in advance, before your child spends time and money applying to a particular school that will <u>NEVER</u> be able to give you the money you need to send your child to that college.

Question #2 - **Does your school have a standard "unmet need" formula for students who apply for financial aid?**

If a school says "Yes", you want to know by how much they leave the average student short. For example, if your child has a need of $10,000 at a school and they have an average "unmet need" of 50%, they will probably only award you $5,000, and ask you to come up with the other $5,000 on your own.

Make sure you find this out <u>before</u> you apply. It could end up saving you a lot of time and money!

Question #3 - Does your school have a ceiling on the maximum amount of financial aid a student can qualify for?

Some schools have maximum ceilings of $5,000 per student. If this turns out to be the case, and you are eligible to receive $10,000 -

You're Out Of Luck!

Question #4 - If my financial need remains the same for the next 4 years, will my child receive the same financial aid package in years 2, 3, and 4 at your school?

Many schools will award students a great package the first year to attract them to go to their school.

Then, in years 2, 3, and 4, they offer them a much lower package even though their financial need is the same, since the school knows there is a very slim likelihood that the student will transfer after they've already attended that college for 1 year.

Question #5 - If my family's financial need increases in year 2 at your college, will your financial aid package be adjusted accordingly, or will it remain the same?

Some schools will <u>not</u> adjust a student's financial aid package after the first year.

This becomes a serious problem especially if the family's income drops in the later years of college.

You must know this up front, so you won't have to make a tough decision later.

Question #6 - If my child doesn't apply for financial aid in his/her freshman year of college, can he/she apply for aid in future years?

In some cases, it may make sense for you <u>not</u> to apply for aid for the freshman year, especially if you have not done planning and you have all of your assets in the wrong places.

However, some schools have policies of giving priority consideration to students at the school who are already receiving financial aid.

If this is the school's policy, you may be shut out from getting financial aid for all 4 years.

Find this out <u>before</u> you apply!

Question #7 - Does your school have a "cut-off" date for guaranteeing that a student will receive financial aid?

If they do, make sure you get your financial aid forms in <u>before</u> their cut-off date, or there's a good chance you won't get any financial aid!

Question #8 - What is your school's policy on packaging outside scholarships into a financial aid award package?

Some schools will replace the FREE money you found with FREE money they were going to award you. So, in effect, <u>you gain nothing</u> by finding an outside scholarship.

Other schools will allow the outside scholarship to replace the loan money they were going to give you.

Obviously, it's better if they replace loan money rather than FREE money.

Make sure you find out each school's policy before you apply.

***

Failure to ask colleges any of these 8 Vital Questions could end up costing you a lot of time, money, and frustration.

Make sure you take the time to ask each school these 8 questions.

I promise you, it will pay off!

Chapter #7

"What You Must Do <u>After</u> You Fill Out Your College Financial Aid Forms...

And Why It's Still Not Too Late To Increase Your Eligibility For College Funding!"

If it's after January of your child's senior year, you may be finished filling out your FAFSA and Financial Aid Profile forms.

There's only one slight catch...

You're Not Done Yet!

You see, even after you file your financial aid forms, there are still several more "steps" you need to complete.

To begin with, about 4 - 6 weeks after you file your FAFSA, you will receive a multi-page document from the Federal processing center called the "Student Aid Report," or "SAR".

The SAR is basically a computerized print out of all the personal and financial questions you answered on the FAFSA.

Typically, there are two sections to the SAR.

Section One gives you instructions for making changes, and lets you know if you've made any mistakes that need to be corrected when filing out the FAFSA.

Part One of your SAR will also tell you if you qualify for a Pell Grant.

Don't worry if you don't and your SAR says you're ineligible. Most middle class and upper-middle class families DON'T qualify for a Pell Grant since this is a Federal grant that is only meant for low-income families.

If you do happen to qualify for the Pell Grant program, you will have three sections to your SAR, with section three serving as your "voucher" for the Pell Grant program.

Regardless of whether or not you're eligible for the Pell Grant program, your SAR will also tell you your "Expected Family Contribution" which is how much the government expects you to pay towards your child's college education.

Look on the first page of your SAR below the date in small type there are three letters followed by some numbers.

Here's a sample of what it looks like:

Feb. 18, 2001
EFC: 07480

What this means is that according to the Federal formulas, the government expects you to contribute $7,480 towards the first year of college for your child.

Unfortunately, the Federal EFC is <u>not</u> the number most private colleges and universities use. Most of the schools that asked you to fill out a Financial Aid Profile form will be using a different formula to calculate how much you should be paying towards college costs called the "Institutional Methodology." This figure is normally higher than the Federal EFC.

Here's What You Need To Do If You Have To Revise Or Update Your Information...

If you estimated your income and tax information when you originally filled out your financial aid forms, you must revise or update your information as soon as possible.

Since most people don't file their tax returns until April 15th, it would be a good idea to meet with your accountant or tax preparer and explain that you need to update your income tax information on your child's financial aid forms immediately.

Tell your accountant you can't wait until April 15th, or it will hurt your chances of receiving financial aid. This should do the trick.

Anyway, after you've received your final updated income and tax information, it's time to correct it on your SAR.

Go to Part Two of your SAR where it says:

You Told Us:/The Correct Answer Is:

Look for the questions you estimated when you filed your FAFSA and update the information under "The correct answer is" side.

Once you've completed this process, you should call the Financial Aid Offices at all of the colleges you applied to, and they will tell you to do one of three things:

1. Make changes to Part Two of your SAR, and send the revisions to the processing center listed in Part Two of your SAR.

2. Make changes to Part Two of your SAR, and send them directly to the financial aid office.

3. Send the entire SAR with no changes to the financial aid office, and they will make the revisions.

When you speak to the financial aid officers, ask if they want an original copy of the SAR.

If they do, I recommend requesting a duplicate copy of the SAR by calling (319) 337-5665.

Within 2 - 4 weeks after you send Part Two of your revised SAR in, you should receive a totally new updated version of your original SAR with all of your changes. When you receive it, take a close look at it to make sure they made all the necessary changes.

After you've updated your SAR, the next step is to wait to hear back from each of the schools your child is accepted to in the form of an award letter.

Several of the schools will also require you to send in a completed copy of your tax return before they will give you a financial aid package.

In light of this, I highly recommend you get your taxes done as soon as humanly possible.

Also, some financial aid forms will be randomly selected for "verification" which is the equivalent of being selected for an audit by the IRS.

If you are selected for verification, you will be asked to supply a copy of your tax return, and documentation on the income and assets you listed.

But, don't worry if you are selected for verification. It is very commonplace, and a lot less intrusive than an IRS Audit.

If you follow the step-by-step plan I've outlined above, everything should proceed smoothly and award letters will start arriving around April or May.

Chapter #8

"How To Take Control Of The College Funding Process And Get The Maximum Amount Of Money For Your Child's College Education...

In this chapter, we're going to talk about two families - The Greens and The Smiths.

Both families started out with roughly the same financial situation, and their children applied to the same colleges since they both had B averages and 1,100 on their SAT's.

However, that is where the similarities end.

The Greens started to think about the college funding process around December of their son, Timothy's, senior year of high school.

John and Mary Green had a combined income of $60,000, $40,000 in savings, a home worth approximately $150,000, and a rental property worth $60,000.

They had also put $20,000 in savings into Timothy's name because their accountant told them they would save money on taxes.

They waited until January and filled out the financial aid forms themselves.

They got their Student Aid Report (this is what the government sends you after you file a financial aid form) back around the middle of February.

Much to their surprise, this complicated report told them the following things: (1) They had made several mistakes in filling out the financial aid forms and now needed to re-file a new set of forms with the corrected information; (2) It also said their family contribution (the minimum amount they would have to pay at any school) was $18,000.

John and Mary stared at the report in amazement.

John exclaimed, "You mean to tell me that two average folks making a modest income with very little savings have to pay this much? Where in the world do they expect us to get all this money from?

We're already up to our eyeballs in bills, and our savings was supposed to be for retirement - How in the world are we going to send Timothy to college?"

What the Greens weren't aware of was that financial aid is awarded on a first come, first served basis. Since they had to re-submit the financial aid forms, they lost valuable time and ended up losing a lot of college funding.

Around April, Timothy started getting award letters back from the colleges he had applied to.

He got his first one back from Ithaca College, and said to his parents, "This can't be! The government report said we would have to pay $18,000, but this award letter says we have to come up with $22,000. But that's not the worst of it! The money they did offer us is almost all loans with the exception of a $500 grant - How in the world are you guys ever going to be able to afford to send me to college?"

Timothy got the rest of his award letters from the other schools. Unfortunately, most of them were just as bad as Ithaca College.

The Greens had a tough decision to make - should they tell Timothy they couldn't afford to pay for his college education, or should they sacrifice.

They decided to use their life's savings to pay for the first year, and then they would take out a home equity loan to help pay for years 2, 3, and 4.

* * *

The story of the Smith's turned out a lot differently.

They also had a combined income of $60,000, savings of $40,000, a home worth $150,000, and a rental property.

However, they decided to take control of the process.

Mr. Smith decided to use a local college-funding expert who explained the process to him and his wife and told him how to increase his eligibility for financial aid.

The first thing he told the Smith's to do was set up their savings and investments in the most favorable terms legally allowable before filling out the financial aid forms.

The next thing the college funding expert showed them was how to properly value their home for the financial aid forms. He explained that the government uses a special formula called the "Housing Index Multiplier" which is based on the year you purchased your home, and the purchase price. Most people have no earthly idea what this formula is, and end up <u>over</u>-<u>valuing</u> their home, which hurts their eligibility for funding.

The next thing the expert showed the Smiths was which schools their son, Peter, had the best shot of getting money from.

He explained how some schools have a lot of money to give out while others have virtually nothing.

The expert said "You <u>must</u> know which schools can give you the most money <u>before</u> you apply - not after. This way you won't be surprised at the end of the year."

The third thing the expert helped them with was filling out the forms. The Smiths were amazed when he told them that over 90% of all forms go in with errors or inconsistencies. He went on to say, "If your form goes in wrong, you have to re-submit it <u>again</u> and you will lose thousands in funding."

Joe and Cindy Smith wondered whether all of this planning would pay off.

The first good sign was when they received their Student Aid Report. It said their family contribution was only $8,000. This was $10,000 less than what the Greens had to pay - all because the Smiths took control of the process <u>before</u> they filed their forms.

They also discovered that their forms went in "error-free" so they wouldn't have to re-submit any forms.

But the best was yet to come.

Their son, Peter, started to get his award letters back from the colleges he applied to.

He had also applied to Ithaca. Except, unlike Timothy, Ithaca said he would only have to pay the amount of his family contribution, and they would cover all expenses above and beyond that. He also received mostly grant money and only one loan.

Peter also started receiving award letters from the rest of the schools, and the monies offered were almost exactly what the expert told him to expect.

Joe and Cindy had an easy decision to make. All they had to do was come up with their family contribution, and most of the schools covered the rest of the expenses.

Peter ended up going to Ithaca, and his parents didn't have to spend their life's savings or mortgage their house to the hilt to do it.

The Smiths lived happily ever after.

* * *

What was the difference between these two families?

On the surface, they both looked the same. They had similar incomes, assets, and both students had similar grades and SAT scores.

The only difference was that The Smith's took control of the process instead of sitting back and hoping for the best.

Don't put yourself or your family in the same position as The Greens!

Chapter #9

"How To Negotiate The Best Deal On A College Education For Your Child..."

In this chapter, we're going to discuss an extremely important topic - one that will significantly impact both your child and your bank account.

I'm talking about...

How To Negotiate The Best Deal On A College Education!

Most parents take this subject lightly, and figure whatever the schools end up offering them is the best that they will get.

Let me tell you something...

Nothing Could Be Further From The Truth!

Let me ask you a question...when you went to purchase or lease your car - did you accept the first offer they made you, or did you look at their price as a "starting point" for negotiation?

What about when you bought your home? Did you purchase it at list price, or did you muster up all of your negotiating skills to try to get the seller to come down in price?

So why is college any different?

Even the cheapest state schools today will cost you about $14,000 between tuition, fees, books, room and board, and miscellaneous expenses.

A private university can easily cost you $30,000 a year and up.

Now multiply those amounts by 4. Wow!!! And that doesn't even include graduate school (God forbid!).

Are you starting to get my point yet?

A college education for your child (or children) is one of the single biggest investments you will ever make in your entire lifetime!

Doesn't it make sense to treat it like any other major purchase, and do your best to negotiate the best possible financial aid package for your child?

So Where Do You Begin?

Well, for starters, your children should be doing their best to get good grades in school. In addition, they should be taking some type of review course to get a good score on their SAT's/ACT's (it's a little late for seniors, but <u>not</u> for juniors).

Second, you must start narrowing down your school choices to colleges and universities where your child lies in the top 25% of the applicant pool - this will significantly increase your chances of getting a good financial aid package.

Next, you must start researching schools that have the best policies on giving good financial aid packages. You want your child to apply to schools that will meet most or all of your family's financial need. It is also important to pick schools that have a history of giving more FREE money, less loans.

<u>Hint</u> - Pick schools that are well endowed and have a lot of money to give out to students. Private schools tend to have far more money available than state schools do. I recommend picking a couple of state schools as "safety" schools and the rest should be well-endowed private schools.

Fourth, you must apply to, at least, 6 - 8 schools to insure that your child gets a good offer from 1 or 2 of them. If all the schools are of the same academic caliber, and some give you a good financial aid package while others give you poor packages - it will allow you to pit one college against the other when negotiating for a better financial aid package. Schools of equal caliber will often times compete for the same student by offering aggressive financial aid packages. Be sure to take advantage of this.

Lastly, you must know your numbers in advance.

For example, do you know what your "Expected Family Contribution" is?

It is the minimum amount that the government expects you to pay towards ANY school.

Schools determine what they are going to offer you by subtracting your Family Contribution from their "Cost of Attendance".

This provides them with your family's "Financial Need".

Frequently, schools will offer parents far less than what they were eligible to receive. Most families don't dispute this since they have no idea of what they should have been offered in the first place.

Don't Let This Happen To You!

Know your numbers in advance.

Find out what your Expected Family Contribution is. Then, find out what the cost of attendance is at each school.

Make sure the schools include all costs such as tuition, fees, books, room and board, living expenses, transportation, and miscellaneous expenses.

Once you get these two numbers, calculate your financial need at each school, and make sure their financial aid packages meets most or all of your need.

If they don't, call or write the school to discuss why they "left you short", and try to create a subtle competition with other schools your child applied to.

If you follow these steps, you should have no problem getting a great package from, at least, 2 or 3 of the schools your child applied to.

Chapter #10

WARNING!!!

"Failure To Understand The New Tax Breaks Under The Current Tax Code Could Be Hazardous To Your Wealth!"

Here's Your Quick Start Guide To The Educational Benefits Of The 2001 Tax Law...

The Economic Growth and Tax Relief Reconciliation Act was passed in June, 2001.

And like many tax bills, this act makes a horribly complicated situation even more complex!

The last reform in 1997 filled the tax laws with loopholes, pitfalls, and financial minefields. This reform adds a few more and throws in time limits for luck.

First though, the good news. There *are* a number of new benefits available for families paying college tuition fees:

- **Withdrawals from qualified state tuition programs (like Section 529 plans) are now tax-free**. You also have more control over these plans. Instead of having to both transfer funds to a different plan *and* change the beneficiary if you want to avoid tax penalties, you can now simply switch plans penalty-free once a year.

- **Coverdell ESA's (the old Education IRA's) are bigger.** Instead of being capped at $500, beneficiaries under the age of 18 can now receive up to $2,000 per year. There's no tax deduction for the contribution, but the tax is deferred on the fund's growth, and withdrawals are tax-free for qualified expenses. (These expenses have been expanded to include computers and internet access.) There's also a useful loophole in this law: while there are income limits for high-earning contributors, anyone can contribute, including lower-earning relatives.

- **The "Hope Credit" remains untouched.** Parents will still be able to receive a 100% tax credit on the first $1,000 of each child's tuition fees for the first two years, and a 50% credit for the next $1,000 worth of expenses in the same period.

- **The "Lifetime Learning Credit" has been increased.** The 20% tax credit on the first $5,000 of tuition fees after the second year has been increased to $10,000 of education expenses every year. (It's important to note that both these credits are calculated according to "out-of-pocket" expenses. Scholarships and grants may reduce the credit; loans may not.)

    It's important to note that these two credits will be phased out for single filers with incomes between $41,000 and $51,000, and joint filers with incomes between $82,000 and $102,000 and you can only use one credit per student.

- **There is a new deduction of up to $4,000 for educational expenses.** You can take this deduction even if you don't itemize your deductions, or you have an Adjusted Gross

Income (AGI) of less than $65,000 for a single parent or $130,000 for a couple filing jointly. On the downside, if you do take this deduction, you can't take the Hope or Lifetime Learning Credit for the same student in the same year. (You're probably better off taking the education credits if you can, but you should definitely get the advice of a professional college funding advisor to see which is best for you.)

- **Deductions for the interest paid on qualified student loans have been expanded.** The interest deductions have been raised to $2,500 and the deduction will no longer be limited to the first 60 months of interest payments.

That's the good news.

There's also a fair amount of bad news:

- **First, all these benefits come with a sale-by date.** Some provisions in the law only last a few years (the new $4,000 deduction, for example, ends in 2006.) As things stand now, the *entire tax code* will be invalid after Dec. 31, 2010. That's definitely something to consider if you've got more than one child heading to college over the next few years.

- **Some middle-income families may be cut out of many of the new benefits.** If you earn more than $50,000 (or $100,000 for joint filers), for example, you won't get the full $2,500 of student loan interest deductions. If your income is over $65,000 (or $130,000 for joint filers), you won't get *any* of these deductions.

- **Timing is crucial.** Because your eligibility for some of these deductions will depend on the tax year you make the payments, you'll have to plan all your college payments very carefully. Pay a tuition fee too early, and you could find yourself unable to claim a tax credit!

- **You can't win them all!** Applying for one credit may well make you ineligible for another. The same child, for example, cannot earn you both a Hope Credit and a Lifetime Learning Credit in the same year. Nor can you claim either of these credits for expenses paid with money pulled out of 529 Plans or Coverdell ESA's.

- **Most importantly, many of these benefits will have an effect on your EFC.** Picking up a Hope Credit or Lifetime Learning Credit, for example, will leave you with more untaxed income. That means colleges may lower their financial aid packages. You should still end up paying less money, but you'll need to figure out precisely how much.

* * *

Whew!

Pretty confusing stuff, huh?

The truth is...

Most CPA's And Tax Preparers Don't Have A Clue About The Educational Provisions Of The New Tax Law!

Where does that leave you as a parent of a college-bound student?

Up the creek if you don't understand how each of these provisions applies to you, and which credit is best to take and when.

One of the results of the new tax law is that individual advice has become more important than ever.

One solution will *not* fit all!

The way parents of college children arrange their finances to pay tuition fees will now vary more widely than ever from one family to another.

The only way to make sure you're not paying more than you need for your child's education is to sit down with a qualified college funding expert and find the best financial arrangement for you!

Chapter #11

"How To Get Maximum Money For College If You're Divorced, A Minority, Own A Business, Recently Unemployed, Or The Parent Of An Athlete..."

In this chapter, we're going to talk about special topics or circumstances if your family situation doesn't fit into the "norm".

What I mean by the "norm" is...married, average student, average grades, employed by a company (not your own), non-minority, etc. You get the point.

Anyway, most families, in one way or another, don't fit into the statistical norm, and must be aware of how this will affect their chances of qualifying for financial aid.

So without further ado, let's talk about...

**Vital Things You Must Know If You Fit Into
One Or More Of The Following Categories:**

<u>Category #1</u> - Divorced Or Separated Parents.

If you are currently divorced or separated (or will be soon), and your child will be applying to colleges next year, there are a few key things you should be aware of:

1. The financial aid forms should be completed by the parent with whom the student lives for the greater part of the year. For example, if a child lives with his mother for 8 months out of the year and with his father only 4 months, the income and asset information should be based on the mother <u>only</u>.

2. If the parent with whom the child resides is remarried, you <u>must</u> include the income and the assets of the stepparent as if he or she was the biological parent. This may not sound fair, but this is the way the financial aid formulas work.

3. Private colleges and universities <u>can</u> ask to see the income and asset information of the "other" divorced parent when awarding their own funds. However, this information will <u>not</u> affect federally based funds.

Category #2 - Academically Or Athletically Gifted Students, And Minorities.

Although most financial aid is based on "need", it is also important to remember that financial aid packages are based to some extent on how badly colleges <u>need</u> your child.

There are three major areas that you should pay close attention to when applying for financial aid:

1. **<u>Academically Gifted Students</u>** - One of the primary scholarships awarded based on academic merit is the National Merit Scholarship Program. It is given to students who do extremely well on their PSAT/ NMSQT scores. Also, many schools (outside of the Ivy League) try to attract top students away from the more highly rated schools by offering academic scholarships. If your child is academically gifted, use this as a bargaining chip.

2. **<u>Athletes</u>** - Even if your child is not Division #1 sports material, don't assume that Division #2 or #3 schools won't offer you preferential packaging (more grants, less loans) to attract your child to their school. Make sure you get in touch with the athletic department and make it a point to meet the coach at each school you visit. Also, get the high school coach to write letters of recommendation to each school.

3. **Minorities** - If your child is Black,
   Hispanic, or Native American, contact the
   colleges and find out about the availability
   of scholarship programs for minorities.
   Although there is some debate over
   awarding these types of scholarships,
   colleges in 19 states currently make these
   types of awards.

Category #3 - Owning Your Own Business.

If you currently own your own business, or you
are thinking of starting one, there are significant
benefits when it comes to getting money for
college.

To begin with, business assets are counted <u>much
less</u> heavily than personal assets.

Also, you have the ability to control (or lower)
your income during the years that your child is in
college, thereby making you eligible for more
financial aid.

All in all, owning or starting a business can be a
big help in getting money for college.

Category #4 - Recently Unemployed.

If you were recently terminated, or have received notice that you will be terminated, or if you own your own business and cannot make a living due to current economic conditions, you must make the college financial aid officer aware of this.

There is something called "professional judgment" that a financial aid officer can use to help you out in this situation.

Most frequently, what they can do for you is use "expected income" rather than the previous year's income which is more reflective of your current financial state.

Category #5 - Independent Students.

For those of you who plan to try to make your child appear to be "independent" so you can get more financial aid, you're in for a shock!

There are 6 criteria that will be used to determine whether or not your child will be considered independent:

1. They will be 24 years of age or older before December 31st of their 1st year of college.

2. They are a veteran of the armed forces.

3. They are an orphan or ward of the court.

4. They have legal dependents.

5. They are a graduate or professional student.

6. They are married.

If your child doesn't fit into one of the above criteria, forget about trying to prove that they are independent - it won't work!

Category #6 - Applying For Early Decision.

If you plan to apply for financial aid, I have only one recommendation concerning applying for early decision...

Don't Do It!

If your child gets accepted to a school for early decision, they must go to that school even if they offer you a horrible package. The school is also aware of this which gives them an incentive to "under-award" you.

If you still decide to apply for early decision, just be forewarned.

* * *

Chapter #12

"5 Little-Known Secrets To Paying For College If You Don't Get Enough Financial Aid..."

In this chapter, we're going to talk about innovative payment options just in case you didn't get enough money for your child's college education.

Or, if you're the parent of a high school Junior, these payment options will help you to understand where to turn if the schools let you down and you still need more money for college.

Well, one thing's for certain...

It's Getting Tougher & Tougher To Get A Great Financial Aid Package From Colleges These Days!

Why Is This?

To begin with, colleges and universities are receiving less money from the Federal and State governments.

There is also a trend towards <u>less</u> FREE money and more loans being given out to help fund a college education.

All of these things have led to students receiving less money than they <u>should be</u> entitled to under the financial aid formulas.

Some schools, particularly the private universities, have more flexibility when it comes to negotiating for a better financial aid package, while others, like state colleges, have very little room to do anything.

This means it is imperative for you as a parent to understand <u>ALL</u> of the payment options available to you just in case the college your child is dying to go to comes up short when awarding you financial aid.

So, without further ado...

<u>Here Are The 5 Little-Known Secrets To Paying For College If You Don't Get Enough Financial Aid</u>:

<u>Secret #1</u>: Have Your Child Start Out At A State School And Then Transfer To A Private College.

If your child gets accepted to both private universities and state schools, and he/she prefers to go to one of the private schools - the first thing you need to look at is how much is it really going to cost you to send him/her to that school.

If the private university offers you an excellent package, which makes it approximately the same cost to you whether you send your child to private, or state - the answer seems pretty simple - send your child to their top choice.

If, however, the private university offers you a less-than-competitive package, and sending your child there will put you deep into debt, my recommendation is to think about sending him/her to a state school for two years, and then have them transfer over to a private university.

You will probably end up saving yourself about $30,000, and your child will end up with a diploma from a private university to boot.

However, I must caution you: If your son/ daughter doesn't plan to get top grades (A- or above) at the state school, they're going to have a tough time transferring over to a top private university.

Also, schools tend <u>NOT</u> to offer their best packages to transfer students.

Keep these things in mind before you opt to take advantage of this.

Secret #2: **Think About Sending Your Child To A College That Offers Cooperative Education.**

About 900 colleges and universities across the country offer programs where students can alternate between full-time study, and a full-time job.

This differs from work/study in that work/study jobs tend to be part-time jobs that students work at for a couple of hours a day until they've earned the amount of the award.

On the other hand, cooperative education offers periods of full-time employment in jobs that the student is interested in pursuing after they graduate.

The student usually makes enough money to pay for a good portion of tuition, and they have a much better chance of landing a good job after they graduate.

The only downfall is it will probably take 5 years to graduate.

Secret #3: **Have Your Child Take The Military Route.**

There are two different options here.

The first one is the Reserve Officer Training Corps. which has branches at many colleges. To qualify for an ROTC Scholarship which usually covers full or partial tuition plus $100 a month allowance, your child must apply in his/her senior year of high school. They should also have good grades and 1200 or above SAT scores.

The other option is applying to one of the service academies, which are extremely difficult to get into. To apply, your child must have excellent grades and SAT scores, pass a physical, and have a recommendation from a Congressman or Senator. If your child can get past all of the above, they will enjoy a FREE college education.

The only downside to going the military route is your child will be required to serve several years in the military after they graduate.

Secret #4: Look Into Outside Scholarships To Help Pay For College.

True, private scholarships only make up 3% of all monies available for paying for college. But, you definitely won't get <u>any</u> of this money if you don't apply for it.

<u>Caution</u> - Don't just use any old scholarship search company or even worse internet searches that promise millions of dollars of unclaimed scholarships. Most of these search services are bogus and will charge you an arm and a leg for their service.

Secret #5: Try Borrowing From An Innovative Loan Program.

Before you look into any type of loan programs, do your best to qualify for federally subsidized loans, which are interest-free and principal free until your child graduates.

If you still need to borrow more money, try borrowing from your 401k plan or a pension plan. Many plans will allow you to borrow up to 50% of the value of the plan or up to $50,000 interest-free.

You should also think about taking out a home equity loan instead of a commercial loan since all of your interest payments will be tax deductible.

* * *

Chapter #13

"A Treasure Chest Of Tips To Beat The High Cost Of College..."

I think you're really going to love this section!

Rather than covering just one strategy or technique to beat the high cost of college, I'm going to share with you...

"A Bushel Of Unusual Tips And Strategies to Beat The High Cost Of College!"

We have a lot to cover in this section, so without further ado - let's get started:

1. Choose Colleges That Have Innovative Payment Plans. Don't only pay attention to the normal college search criteria like courses offered, academic and athletic reputation, geographic location, etc. Instead, make sure you inquire about special scholarships, installment plans, guaranteed cost plans, and tuition remission for good grades. Remember, if you don't ask - they won't tell!

2. Always Apply To, At Least, Two Or Three Schools That Are Rated Equally. This way, if your child gets accepted to all of them, you may be able to play one against the other when negotiating to get a better financial aid package.

3. Try To Understand The Financial Aid Formulas. By understanding the formula, you will start to see how different factors will affect your eligibility for financial aid. For example, "Should you move the assets out of your child's name?" or "Should Mom or Dad take two courses at a local community college to qualify as a part-time student?" By knowing the formula in advance of applying, you can legally set up your personal and financial situation to maximize your eligibility for financial aid.

4. Send Your Child To A Community College For His/Her First Two Years Of School. If your child works hard and gets good grades, they can usually transfer to a top private university. This way, they can get a diploma from a prestigious school for half the cost!

5. Check Out Your State's Financial Aid Programs. By contacting your state's higher education agency, you can find out what financial aid programs they can offer "in-state" students. Many states have grant and low-interest loan programs specifically to help students who plan to pursue careers in medicine or teaching. Check with your state agency to see what they have for your child!

6. Don't Say "No" To Subsidized Student Loans.
If you end up qualifying for either a Perkins loan or
a subsidized Stafford loan, think very strongly about
taking it! These loans are interest-free for the four
years your child is in school and up to six months
after they graduate. In effect, the government is
picking up the tab on these loans for four entire
years. You may even be able to borrow the money,
gain interest on it for four years, and then pre-pay
the loan after four years without paying any interest
whatsoever. Check with your lender to find out.

**7. Have Your Child Complete Four Years Of
College In Three Years.** Your child will have to
attend summer school, but you will save the 7 - 8%
increase in tuition for the fourth year.

**8. File Your Financial Aid Forms Accurately
And On Time.** Remember, financial aid is awarded
on a first come, first served basis. If you submit
your forms with errors or omissions, it will
probably "bump" the financial aid forms, and you
will have to resubmit them at a later time. If this
happens, you will probably lose aid since they
award money on a first come, first served basis.
Also, make sure to get your forms in on time. Most
schools have different deadlines, and if you miss
their deadline, you will almost definitely get less
funding. The moral of the story is - File your forms
correctly the first time!

9. Pick Colleges That Have The Best Histories Of Giving Good Financial Aid Packages. Many schools publish statistics on how much "need" they meet and how much FREE money and loans they give out. Know these numbers before you apply, so you don't waste time and money applying to schools you'll never be able to afford.

10. Don't Be Afraid To Negotiate For A Better Financial Aid Package. A school's financial aid package is <u>NOT</u> fixed in stone. Just because they offer you a certain package, doesn't mean you have to accept it. If you know how to calculate your "expected family contribution" and you find out what the school's history of giving out financial aid is, you can usually get a pretty accurate idea of what you should have received. If the school's offer is way off - write a letter to negotiate. I have seen <u>many</u> cases where schools gave $2,000... $3,000... even $6,000 more than they originally offered just because the family asked. The moral is - Don't Be Afraid To Negotiate!

11. If You Can't Afford To Pay Your "Expected Family Contribution", Think About Taking Out A Home Equity Loan Or Line Of Credit. By taking out a home equity loan instead of a commercial loan, your interest payments will be tax-deductible, and you will be reducing the value of your home for financial aid purposes. Although the federal formulas no longer ask about home equity, many private colleges still include it when determining how much money they will give you.

12. Have Your Child Enroll In Advanced Placement Classes Or Enroll In College Level Courses While They're Still In High School. Every college level course they place out of is money you won't have to pay when they go to college. Considering college credits can cost as much as $300 each, having your child place out of these courses can save you a lot of money.

13. Have Your Child Pick A College That Offers Cooperative Education. There are over 900 colleges and universities that offer these kinds of programs. Your child will alternate taking classes with working in a job that is related to the career they want to pursue. It may take an extra year for them to finish college, but they will have a much better chance of landing a good job when they graduate.

14. Be Sure To Apply For Financial Aid Even If You Don't Think You'll Be Eligible. Most families that make between $50,000 - $150,000 per year and own a home do qualify for some forms of financial aid. Sadly, many parents are under the misconception that they won't qualify so they don't even try. This is a huge mistake since you definitely won't be offered any money if you don't apply. Even if you don't qualify based on financial "need", many schools won't even consider you for "non-need" based aid if you don't try applying for need-based aid. So, regardless of what you've been told - give it a shot and apply!

<u>Don't Spend A Lot Of Your Time Looking For Private Scholarships</u>. Private scholarships from foundations and organizations <u>only</u> make up approximately 3% of all the funding out there. The other 97% comes from the Federal Government, the state you live in, and the colleges or universities your child applies to. Spend most of your time applying for the 97%, instead of wasting a lot of time going after the 3%!

Chapter 14

Special Bonus Section

"9 New Secrets To Beating The High Cost Of College"

I know you're the parent of a college-bound student, and you're probably wondering how in the world you are going to pay for it! You have every right to be concerned since the average cost of a 4-year college education today is between $50,000-$160,000.

If you're like most folks, you'll probably end up mortgaging your house to the hilt, or spending your entire life's savings to muster up enough money to send your child to college. Or, <u>even worse</u>, if you don't have a lot of home equity or money in the bank, you'll end up sending your child to the least expensive school <u>rather</u> than the best college they can get into.

Either way, you'll probably end up feeling <u>guilty</u>, <u>frustrated</u>, and <u>angry</u> when you have to tell your child the truth - "I just can't afford to send you to the college of your choice, you'll have to settle for a state university or local community college."

What if I told you that, in most cases, you don't have to make these painful decisions. . .

Here's The Good News. . .

My name is Daniel Wansten. I am the founder of Professional Education Services, one of the leading college financial counseling services in the nation.

I _guarantee_ you will discover how to beat the high cost of college!

I know this sounds too good to be true, but it really is possible! In fact, many families discover they can send their child to an expensive private university for less than the cost of a state college!

I guess you're wondering why I'm telling you all of this? The answer is quite simple. We have personally helped parents like you to send their children to expensive private and state universities that they never thought they could afford...

And There's A Good Chance I Can Do The Same For YOU!

Because you took the time to read this book, I am offering you 1 FREE hour of my personal time (a value of $220).

During Your FREE $220 Consultation, I Will Reveal These "9 New Secrets To Beating The High Cost Of College":

<u>Secret #1</u>. <u>Why Some Middle-Class and Upper-Middle Class Parents Pay Close To Nothing For Their Children's College Educations!</u>

Most middle and upper-middle class parents automatically assume they won't be eligible for financial aid if they make over $60,000 per year, and they own a home.

In most cases, these parents are eligible for some forms of financial aid since the formulas also take into consideration the total number of family members, how many of these family members will be attending college at the same time, the cost of the colleges and universities being applied to, etc. Don't assume you won't be eligible.

I have even discovered a way for higher income, higher tax bracket families earning well over $150,000 a year to pay for college ...*on a tax favored basis.*

Secret #2. Why Some High School "Financial Aid Nights" And Some High School Guidance Counselors Can Be Hazardous To Your Wealth!

Many parents unknowingly assume that all of their concerns will be answered at the high school "Financial Aid Night" or by their child's guidance counselor. Unfortunately, this rarely turns out to be the case.

Guidance counselors care about your kids but they are over worked and often they are too bogged down dealing with issues such as teenage pregnancy, drugs, helping students pick colleges, etc. to devote the adequate amount of time necessary to help each and every individual parent apply for financial aid.

Financial Aid Nights primarily focus on how to fill out the forms.

They do not explain how to legally and ethically increase your eligibility for financial aid by doing "income and asset" planning. They also do not help you pick schools based on each schools ability to give you a good financial aid package.

And lastly, they will not show you how to negotiate to get the best possible financial aid package from each school.

All in all, go to your Financial Aid Night, but **DON'T** expect it to solve all your problems.

Secret #3. How To Send Your Child To An Expensive Private University For Less Than A State School! (This one really amazes my clients!)

Believe it or not, some private schools end up being cheaper than a state school or a local community college.

How can this be you ask?

Let me explain. . .

No matter what school your child applies to, you will have to pay your "Family Contribution", which is the minimum amount of money the government will expect your family to pay at any school.

So let's say your child applies to two schools - one private university and one state college. The private school costs $25,000 per year and the state school costs $10,000 per year.

Let's assume your family contribution is calculated to be $5,000 - which is the minimum the government expects you to pay towards either school.

But here's what happens. Because the private university is well-endowed and has a lot of money to give out, they end up offering you financial aid that will cover all expenses above $5,000 - so all you pay out of pocket to send your child to a $25,000 a year school is $5,000.

Unfortunately, the state school does **NOT** have a lot of money to give out, and all they offer you is $2,000 in aid - so you end up paying $5,000 plus the $3,000 they left you short by for a total of $8,000.

It actually ends up cheaper to send your child to a private school.

Secret #4. **How To Lower Your "Out-of-Pocket" Costs, And Get The Maximum Amount Of Money From Each School ! (Just like a good C.P.A. can minimize your tax liability, I can show you how to set up your financial situation in the most favorable terms legally allowable!)**

Certain assets are counted much more heavily in the financial aid formulas than others. Where you keep your money could mean the difference between getting $10,000 in financial aid or getting nothing. If you don't know how to legally and ethically position your money properly for purposes of financial aid, you could end up losing thousands in financial aid.

Secret #5. How To Pick Colleges That Will Give You The Best Financial Aid Packages - More FREE Money, Less Loans! (Why waste your time applying to schools that will never give you the money you need?)

Some schools are well-endowed and have the ability to award a lot of money to students. Other schools have very little money to give away.

It's important for you to know this information before you ever apply to a school.

By knowing, in advance, which schools give the best financial aid packages, you can have your child pick schools that they have the best shot of getting money from.

This way, you don't waste time and money applying to and visiting schools you will never be able to afford.

Secret #6. How To Fill Out The Complicated Financial Aid Forms Accurately and On-Time! Over 90% Go In With Errors! (If this happens, you will lose most or all of your eligibility for financial aid!)

Did you know that according to the Department of Education, over 90% of all financial aid forms go in with errors or inconsistencies?

Simple mistakes like omitting a social security number, using white-out to make corrections, and not registering a male student for the selective service can actually "bump" a form.

If this happens, you will have to reprocess your financial aid forms which will take another 4-6 weeks.

Since financial aid is awarded on a first come, first served basis, it is imperative that you get your forms in accurately and on time, or you will miss out on thousands of dollars in financial aid that you would have been eligible for.

Secret #7. How To Locate and Apply For Every "Need-Based" Scholarship, Grant, and Low-Interest Loan That Your Child May Be Eligible For!

Leave no stone unturned when searching for money for college. Be sure to apply for all "need-based" sources of funding through the Federal government, the state you live in, and the colleges and universities your child is applying to. Most of these financial aid programs can be applied for by simply filling out the Federal form (the FAFSA) and, in some cases, the Institutional Form (the CSS Financial Aid Profile).

Secret #8. How To Pay For Your Child's Education On A Tax Favored Basis! (I've used this technique to help my higher tax bracket clients who don't qualify for need based financial aid!)

Do you make in excess of $150,000 a year?

If you answered "Yes", there's a good chance you won't qualify for need based aid.

But what if I told you there is a way for you to make college tuition tax deductible? Do you think that might save you some money?

On average, we can show higher income clients how to save over $4,000 a year in taxes!

Secret #9. How To Send Your Child To The College Of Their Choice Without Spending Your Life's Savings Or Paying Out Of Your Current Income!

Just like a good CPA can help you lower your tax liability, a good college funding consultant can help you get more money for your child's college education.

But before you pick a consultant, make sure they offer the following services: (1) Help you arrange your income and assets to lower your "out-of-pocket" costs and increase your eligibility for college aid; (2) Help you pick schools that you have the best shot of getting money from; (3) Help you fill out the two major financial aid forms so they go in accurately and on time; and (4) Help you negotiate with schools to get the best possible aid package.

Not taking advantage of any of these "9 Secrets" could literally cost you thousands of dollars in lost financial aid that you may be eligible to receive. Don't let this happen to you!

* * *

I may or may not have the answer to your college financing problems, but don't you think it's worth a phone call and a couple of minutes of your time to find out! There is no obligation, and if nothing else, you'll learn a great deal about the college financial aid process.

So pick up the phone and call me now. You can reach me at (616) 949-7935. Ask my assistant Michelle to schedule an appointment for you to take advantage of your free gift 1 hour consultation.

My normal business hours are from 9:00 a.m.- 5:00 p.m., Monday-Thursday.

I reserve Fridays for administrative work and I do not have evening hours available.

Why Am I Making You This Generous Offer?

Because I have a feeling that once you see how much money and time I can save you, there's a very good chance that you will end up becoming one of my next happy customers.

Remember, financial aid is awarded on a first come-first served basis. So, it is imperative that you start your planning immediately since waiting can severely limit your chances of receiving the maximum amount of financial aid!

So, pick up the phone and call me now at (616) 949-7935.
I'll be waiting to hear from you.

Sincerely,

Daniel Wansten

The Nations Source for College Funding Advice.

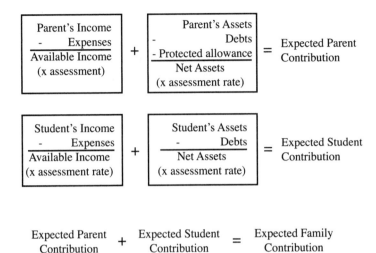

ASSET PROTECTION ALLOWANCE
(approximate)

Age	Two Parent Family	One Parent Family
39 or less	$34,800	$17,400
40-44	$39,200	$19,400
45-49	$44,300	$21,600
50-54	$50,400	$24,200
55-59	$57,900	$27,400
60-64	$67,300	$31,200
65 or more	$74,000	$34,100

GLOSSARY

ACADEMIC YEAR: A measure of academic work to be performed by the student, subject to definition by the school.

ACCESS GROUP: An education and financing organization that distributes and processes the Needs Access financial aid application.

AGI: Adjusted gross income. In 2002, the AGI will be listed on line 35 of the IRS 1040;line 21 of the IRS 1040A and line 4 of the IRS 1040EZ.

AMERICAN COLLEGE TESTING PROGRAM (ACT): A federally approved need analysis service that processes the Free Application for Federal Student Aid (FAFSA). Also the administrator of a group of standardized tests in English, mathematics, reading, and science reasoning.

BASE INCOME YEAR (also known as the BASE YEAR): The calendar year preceding the academic year for which aid is being sought.

BUSINESS/FARM SUPPLEMENT: A supplemental aid application required by a few colleges for aid applicants whose parents own businesses or farms or who are self-employed. The individual school's aid policy will determine if this form must be completed.

CAMPUS-BASED PROGRAMS: Three federal student aid programs that are administered directly by the schools financial aid office (the Perkins loan, the Supplemental Educational Opportunity Grant, and the Federal Work-Study program).

COLLEGE BOARD: A nonprofit association that writes and processes the CSS Financial Aids Profile form.

COOPERATIVE EDUCATION: A college program offered at many schools that combines periods of academic study with periods of paid employment related to the student's field of study. In most cases, participation will extend the time required to obtain a bachelor's degree to five years.

COST OF ATTENDANCE: A figure, estimated by the school that includes the cost of tuition, fees, room board, books and supplies as well as an allowance for transportation and personal expenses. This figure is compared to the Expected Family Contribution to determine a student's aid eligibility. Also known as the *student budget*.

DEFAULT: Failure to repay a loan according to the terms of the promissory note.

DEPENDENT STUDENT: A classification for aid purposes for a student who is considered to be dependent upon his or her parent(s) for financial support.

EXPECTED FAMILY CONTRIBUTION (EFC): The amount of money the family is expected to contribute for the year toward the student's cost of attendance. This figure is compared to the Cost of Attendance to determine a student's aid eligibility.

FAF: See Financial Aid Form.

FAFSA: See Free Application for Federal Student Aid.

FAMILY CONTRIBUTION: Another name used to refer to the Expected Family Contribution.

FAO: See Financial Aid Officer.

FEDERAL METHODOLOGY: The generally accepted method used to calculate the family's expected contribution to college costs for federal aid purposes. Depending on the individual college's policy the federal methodology may also be used to determine eligibility for money under the school's control.

FEDERAL WORK-STUDY (FWS): A federally funded aid program that provides jobs for students Eligibility is based on need.

FINANCIAL AID: A general term used to refer to a variety of program funded by the federal and state governments on well as the individual schools to assist students with their educational costs. While the names may vary, financial aid comes in three basic forms: (1) gift aid (grants and scholarships) which do not have to be paid back (2) student loans, and (3) work-study jobs.

FINANCIAL AID FORM (FAF): A need analysis document that was written and processed by the College Scholarship Service (CSS) in Princeton, New Jersey. The 1995-96 version of the FAF was the last one written.

FINANCIAL AID PROFILE FORM: See PROFILE form.

FINANCIAL AID OFFICER: An administrator at each school who determine whether a student is eligible for aid and if so, the type of aid to awarded.

FREE APPLICATION FOR FEDERAL STUDENT AID (FAFSA): The need analysis document written by U.S. Departments of Education. This form is required for virtually all students seeking financial aid including the unsubsidized Stafford loan.

401 (k), 403 (b): The names of two of the more popular deferred compensation plans in which employees elect to defer part of their earnings until a later date.

GIFT AID: Financial aid, usually a grant or scholarship, that does not have to be paid back and that does not involve employment.

GRANTS: Gift aid that is generally based on need. Federal and state governments as well as the individual schools can fund the program.

GUARNTEED STUDENT LOANS (GSL): See Stafford Student Loan program.

HALF-TIME STATUS: Refers to students taking at least 6 credits per semester or the equivalent.
INDEPENDENT STUDENT: A student who, for financial aid purposes, is not considered dependent on his or her parent(s) for support. Also known as a self-supporting student.

INCOME PROTECTION ALLOWANCE: A deduction against income in both the federal and the institutional methodologies.

ISNTITUIONAL METHODOLOGY: An alternative method used to calculate the family's expected contribution to college cost. This methodology is generally used by private and a few state schools to determine eligibility for aid funds under the school's direct control. Colleges that use the institutional methodology usually require completion of the Profile form.

LONG FORM: This generally refers to the IRS 1040 form.

NATIONAL DIRECT STUDENT LOANS (NDSL): See Perkins Loan program.

NEED: The amount of aid a student is eligible to receive. This figure is calculated by subtracting the Expected Family Contribution from the Cost of Attendance.

NEED ACCESS FINANCIAL AID APPLICATION: A need analysis program operated by the Access Group. It is required by many graduate and professional schools to determine eligibility for institutional aid.

NEED ANALYSIS: The process of analyzing the information on the aid form to calculate the amount of money the student and parent(s) can be expected to contribute toward educational costs.

NEED ANALYSIS FORMS: Aid applications used to calculate the expected family contribution. The most common need analysis forms are: the Free Application for Federal Student Aid (FAFSA) and the Financial Aid PROFILE form. Consult the individual school's financial aid filing requirements to determine which form(s) are required for that particular school.

NONCUSTODIAL PARENT'S STATEMENT: A supplemental aid application required by a few colleges for aid applicants whose parents are separated or divorced or who never married. The individual's school's aid policy will determine if this form must be completed. If required, the noncustodial parent will complete this form. This is generally the parent with whom the child spent the least amount of time in the preceding 12 months prior to completion of the form.

PARENTS' CONTRIBUTION: The amount of money the parent(s) are expected to contribute for the year toward the student's Cost of Attendance.

PARENT LOANS FOR UNDERGRADUATE STUDENTS (PLUS): A federal subsidized educational loan program in which parents can borrow up to the total cost of attendance minus any financial aid received for each child in an undergraduate program. Eligibility is not based on need. The interest is variable, currently with a 9%cap.

STAFFORD STUDEN LOAN (SSL) PROGRAM: Formerly known as the Guaranteed Student Loan (GSL) program, this federally funded program provides low-interest loans to undergraduate students and is administered by a bank or other lending institution, which can sometimes be the college itself. In most cases repayment does not begin until six months after the student graduates or leaves school and there are no interest charges while the student is in school. For now borrowers the interest rate is variable, currently with an 8.25% cap. There are two types of Stafford loans: subsidized Stafford loan is non-need based and can be taken out by virtually all students. In many cases students can elect to let the interest accumulate until after the graduate.

STANDARDIZED FORMS: The generic term used in this book when referring to any need analysis forms that must be sent to processing service. The two most commonly used standardized forms are the U.S. Department of Education's Free Application for Federal Student Aid (FAFSA) and the College Board's CSS/Financial Aid Profile form.

STUDENT AID REPORT (SAR): The multi-page report that is issued who have filed a completed FAFSA.

STUDENT BUDGET: See Cost of Attendance.

STUDENT'S CONTIBUTION: The amount of money the student is expected to contribute for the year toward his or her cost of attendance.

SUBSIDIZED STAFFORD LOAN: See Stafford Student Loan (SSL) program.

SUPPLEMNTAL EDUCATION OPPORTUNITY GRANT: A Federally subsidized educational loan program for independent undergraduate and graduate students. Eligibility was not based on need. This loan program has been phased into the Stafford Loan Program. Previous borrowing limits under this program are now represented by the mandatory unsubsidized portion of the Stafford Loan.

UNIFORM AID SUPPLEMENT: A standardized set of supplemental aid questions developed and utilized by a number of highly selective private colleges.

UNSUBSIDIZED STAFFORD LOAN: See Stafford Student Loan (SSL)

VERIFICATION: A process in which the financial aid office requires additional documentation to verify the accuracy of the information reported on the aid applications.

WORK -STUDY: See Federal Work Study.

Pass along this referral card to the people you would want to help save money for college.

For more information concerning upcoming college funding workshops, or to schedule an appointment for a FREE financial aid consultation,...simply call for more information at (616) 949-7935.

If you would like to have Daniel speak to your High School, or at your Public Library, or Community Group call (616) 949-7935 and ask for my assistant Michelle. Be sure to mention that you got this number from Daniel's book.

So pick up the phone and call me now. You can reach me at (616) 949-7935. Ask my assistant Michelle to schedule an appointment for you to take advantage of your free gift 1 hour consultation.

My normal business hours are from 9:00 a.m.- 5:00 p.m., Monday-Thursday.

I reserve Fridays for administrative work and I do not have evening hours available.

Pass along this referral card to the
people you would want to help save
money for college.

Pass along this referral card to the people you would want to help save money for college.

For more information concerning upcoming college funding workshops, or to schedule an appointment for a FREE financial aid consultation,...simply call for more information at (616) 949-7935.

If you would like to have Daniel speak to your High School, or at your Public Library, or Community Group call (616) 949-7935 and ask for my assistant Michelle. Be sure to mention that you got this number from Daniel's book.

So pick up the phone and call me now. You can reach me at (616) 949-7935. Ask my assistant Michelle to schedule an appointment for you to take advantage of your free gift 1 hour consultation.

My normal business hours are from 9:00 a.m.- 5:00 p.m., Monday-Thursday.

I reserve Fridays for administrative work and I do not have evening hours available.

Pass along this referral card to the people you would want to help save money for college.

For more information concerning upcoming college funding workshops, or to schedule an appointment for a FREE financial aid consultation,...simply call for more information at (616) 949-7935.

If you would like to have Daniel speak to your High School, or at your Public Library, or Community Group call (616) 949-7935 and ask for my assistant Michelle. Be sure to mention that you got this number from Daniel's book.

So pick up the phone and call me now. You can reach me at (616) 949-7935. Ask my assistant Michelle to schedule an appointment for you to take advantage of your free gift 1 hour consultation.

My normal business hours are from 9:00 a.m.- 5:00 p.m., Monday-Thursday.

I reserve Fridays for administrative work and I do not have evening hours available.

Pass along this referral card to the people you would want to help save money for college.

For more information concerning upcoming college funding workshops, or to schedule an appointment for a FREE financial aid consultation,...simply call for more information at (616) 949-7935.

If you would like to have Daniel speak to your High School, or at your Public Library, or Community Group call (616) 949-7935 and ask for my assistant Michelle. Be sure to mention that you got this number from Daniel's book.

So pick up the phone and call me now. You can reach me at (616) 949-7935. Ask my assistant Michelle to schedule an appointment for you to take advantage of your free gift 1 hour consultation.

My normal business hours are from 9:00 a.m.- 5:00 p.m., Monday-Thursday.

I reserve Fridays for administrative work and I do not have evening hours available.

Pass along this referral card to the people you would want to help save money for college.

For more information concerning upcoming college funding workshops, or to schedule an appointment for a FREE financial aid consultation,...simply call for more information at (616) 949-7935.

If you would like to have Daniel speak to your High School, or at your Public Library, or Community Group call (616) 949-7935 and ask for my assistant Michelle. Be sure to mention that you got this number from Daniel's book.

So pick up the phone and call me now. You can reach me at (616) 949-7935. Ask my assistant Michelle to schedule an appointment for you to take advantage of your free gift 1 hour consultation.

My normal business hours are from 9:00 a.m.- 5:00 p.m., Monday-Thursday.

I reserve Fridays for administrative work and I do not have evening hours available.